Natasha's Sketchbook

VALUE

by Natasha Gray

Published by
Heron Books, Inc.
20950 SW Rock Creek Road
Sheridan, OR 97378

heronbooks.com

First Edition © 2020, 2021 Heron Books
All Rights Reserved

ISBN: 978-0-89739-187-0

The Heron Books name and the heron bird symbol are registered trademarks of Delphi Schools, Inc.

Any unauthorized copying, translation, duplication or distribution, in whole or in part, by any means, including electronic copying, storage or transmission, is a violation of applicable laws.

Printed in the USA

15 July 2021

Welcome to Value!

Whether you are a beginner or more advanced student, I hope you find the information in this book easy to understand and useful—and the exercises easy and fun!

The full Sketchbook series includes:

Line, Shape, Value, Color, Texture, and Form, plus an accompanying Glossary of Art Terms.

They are best done in order, but don't have to be. All you need is the decision to be creative and expand on your skills as an artist.

Here's to a wonderful journey!

All my love,

Natasha

Materials needed for this course

Main Exercises

    magazines, books (or internet access)
    phone camera
    printer
    set of graphite pencils
    white paper
    fixative spray
    ruler
    two geometric-shaped objects
    sculpture of a face
    lamp

Additional Exercises

    red filter (red acetate value finder, red glass or red plexiglass)
    piece of card stock or sturdy paper
    scrap paper
    piece of black charcoal, chalk or pastel
    scissors
    rag
    fixative spray
    pencil
    black watercolor
    paintbrush
    watercolor paper
    watercolors

TABLE OF CONTENTS

Introduction — 2

The Value Scale — 4

Contrast — 6

Drawing Pencils — 12

Gradation — 16

Light Source & Shadow — 26

    Light Placement — 27

    Shadow Types — 29

    Light Types — 31

        A Tip on Cast Shadows — 32

Seeing Values — 38

Value Transitions — 42

Color and Value — 50

Two Interesting Artists — 52

Additional Exercises — 55

INTRODUCTION

The word **value** in art refers to how light or dark a color is.

Every painting, drawing or photograph has a variety of dark, intermediate and light elements. These are called values.

The harmony and relationship of these different values can create the illusion of light and shadow, make the artwork look three-dimensional, and contribute to the emotional feel or "atmosphere" of the piece.

For example, in the painting on the next page, Johannes Vermeer has created an intimate atmosphere using a perfect balance of lights and darks.

Great artists throughout history have mastered the use of value, enabling them to create masterpieces that evoke powerful emotions and a sense of harmony in their work.

Although it is easier to notice values when looking at a black and white photograph or drawing, values exist in all art, including full-color works.

As a first step toward learning how value applies to color, in this book we will focus on the study of values as concerns black and white, and the shades between.

Woman Holding a Balance, by Johannes Vermeer

THE VALUE SCALE

A **value scale** is a system of gradually darker shades, from white to black. It can have only a few shades of gray or many. The value scale shown here has eight different values from white to black.

Value scales are used by artists as a tool for getting the different values right in a piece they are working on. And each piece of art can have a different value scale.

For example, if you were drawing an apple sitting in bright daylight, you would need a different value scale than if you were drawing an apple sitting in a closet.

In bright daylight, the scale would have more lighter grays and possibly no black.

The value scale for the closet apple might have no white or light grays at all.

By holding your value scale up to the subject you are drawing and comparing the scale values with the subject's values, you can avoid making areas too light or too dark.

This drawing has 8 different values—a pretty wide range.

A value scale can help you, as an artist, control the viewer's attention and emotion.

An understanding and mastery of value will enable you to create more realistic and dynamic works of art!

CONTRAST

When two or more people or things have a noticeable difference between them, that is called **contrast**.

Contrast is important in visual art, whether that contrast is shown through shapes, colors, directions, sizes or other elements.

Most often, however, contrast in visual art refers to differences in value. The greatest contrast in value is of course between black and white. This is called **high contrast**.

High contrast images use very dark and very light values to achieve a more dramatic effect, whether in a drawing, a painting or a photograph.

Normally, high contrast images convey a more mysterious, sad or nocturnal feeling.

High contrast can also be used to create a more dramatic effect.

This high contrast drawing uses only three values: white, one gray, and black.

The human eye is normally drawn to areas of high contrast, so choosing very different values is also a great tool to direct the viewer's attention.

This high contrast drawing uses four values: white, two tones of gray, and black.

Low contrast images have a wide range of intermediate values only and can be used to create a balanced, calm, dreamy or subdued feeling.

This low contrast image used only light gray tones on the value scale, avoiding white or black.

You can select values according to the effect you want to create in your art.

Let's do This!

You will need:

    magazines, books (or internet access)

Find several photographs or images of artwork with the following characteristics:

- High contrast. Pay attention to the difference between the lightest and darkest tones. Notice what types of emotions you feel are conveyed.

- Low contrast. Notice the lack of extreme difference in values. Notice whether the value scale used is on the lighter side, the darker side, or more in the middle. Again, notice what types of emotions the images communicate to you.

- High contrast elements or sections. These are images in which the artist uses high contrast to emphasize a certain part of the whole image. Think of why the artist wanted to draw attention to that particular object, person or section of the piece.

Let's do This!

You will need:
- friend
- phone camera
- printer

Ask a friend to pose for you for a few photographs. Work only in black and white. Do not use a flash.

Turn off the flash and take several photographs of your friend in a variety of places with very different lighting, such as a dark hallway, by a window, outside in direct sunlight.

Notice the different levels of contrast in the photos.

Now play with the photos using different filters on your phone to change the contrast of your images. Notice how changing the values and contrast changes the emotion conveyed.

Print out your favorite one.

DRAWING PENCILS

Graphite pencils, also called **drawing pencils**, follow the value scale. Although they don't have a true black or white (just various shades of gray), they are still arranged from lightest to darkest.

Drawing pencils are categorized as H (hard) or B (soft). Hard pencils leave thin, light lines. Soft pencils leave broad, dark marks. The higher the number, the harder (H) or softer (B) the graphite.

Pencils in between hard and soft are labeled HB or F (sharpens to a fine point).

If you wanted to make a low contrast, light drawing, you would chose to work mostly within the H category pencils. On the other hand, if you wanted a high contrast image, you would work with the dark shades in the B category and would use the white of the paper as the lightest value.

This wide range of graphite pencils allows artists to make marvelous drawings with a full spectrum of lights and darks.

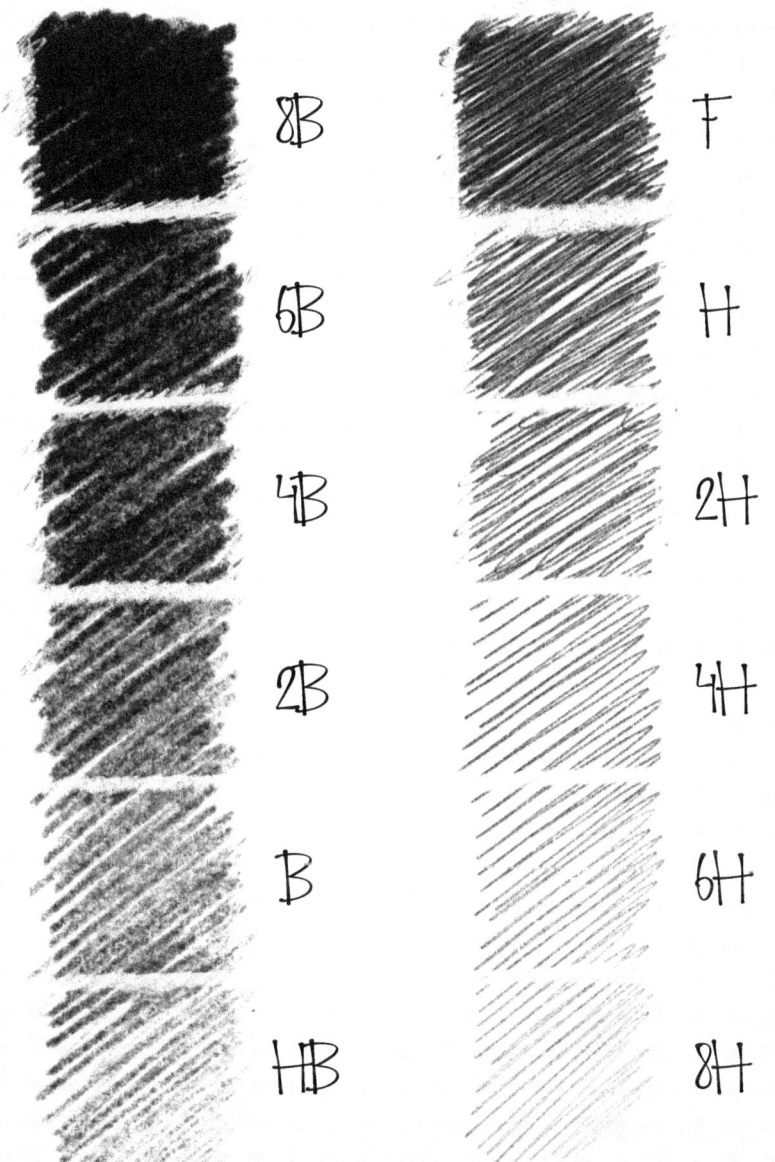

Let's do this!

You will need:
- set of graphite pencils
- white paper
- fixative spray

Draw a 4-inch rectangle and divide it into 1/2-inch sections as shown on the next page. Leave the first section completely white. This is your lightest value. Now color the next part with a very light pencil such as 8H. Fill in the following sections choosing pencils that get progressively darker until your last section is almost black, such as with an 8B pencil.

Write which pencil you used under each section.

Spray it with a fixative.

You now have your own value scale you can keep and use as a guide in making pencil drawings!

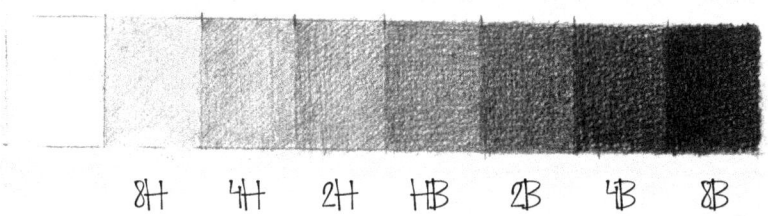

GRADATION

In art, **gradation** is the gradual transition from one color, value, texture or size to another, which can help create the illusion of depth, distance or volume.

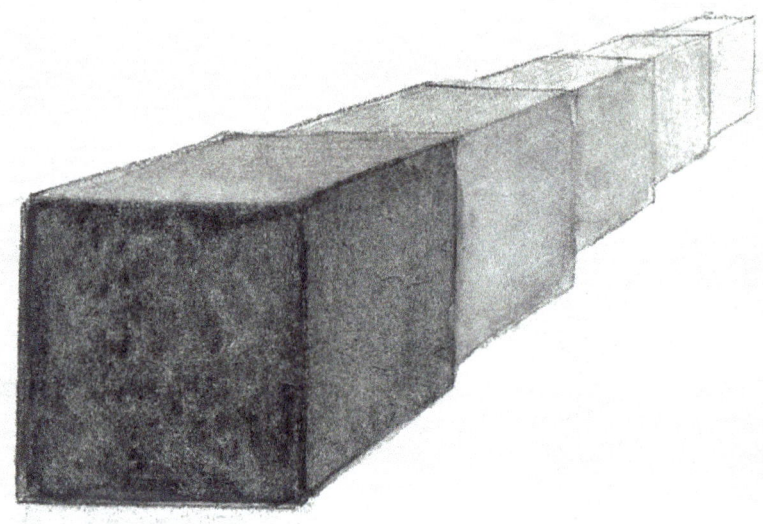

A value scale shows a gradation of values.

In a work of art, values can change suddenly from light to dark, creating a sharp line of contrast—or they can gradually become lighter or darker. When the change is gradual, that is the use of gradation.

Using gradation will help you make objects look more realistic.

Let's do This!

You will need:
- paper
- graphite pencils
- ruler

Draw a 3 x 3 inch square, then divide it into 1-inch sections so that you have 9 squares.

Draw a couple of fun lines inside each one of those squares. They can be curvy or straight.

Now take a light value pencil (one that is in the H range) and shade one of the small sections in a 1-inch square. Then take a slightly darker pencil and shade over the first one, leaving a little bit of the first layer untouched.

Continue doing this until you get to the darkest value at the very end of that small section, working to create a smooth gradation from light to dark.

Repeat this in every shape within that square.

Now move on and repeat this with the other 1-inch squares until you have created a beautiful piece using gradation!

Let's do This!

You will need:
- paper
- ruler
- set of graphite pencils
- your value scale

Using a light pencil, draw four polygons that seem to lay on top of each other in certain sections.

Choose four values to work with. You will be shading in different sections using the four values.

Use the lightest value to shade in the sections of the shapes that don't overlap.

Where two shapes overlap, shade in with the second value.

Where three shapes overlap, shade the sections in with the next darker value.

Where all four shapes overlap, use your darkest value.

Look at the three-dimensional feeling of the drawing!

LIGHT SOURCE & SHADOW

In order to have light and shadow, there must be a light source. This is the place where light is coming from, such as a window, a candle, a light bulb or the sun.

As light shines on an object, it creates specific highlights and shadows which define the shape of the object and give it volume—the illusion of three dimensions. An object will look completely different under different light sources.

The placement of the light source relative to the object will also dramatically change the way the object looks.

Look at the following spheres and observe how much they change depending on where the light source is located.

LIGHT PLACEMENT

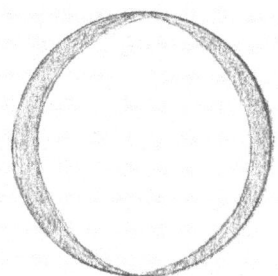

Front light is when the source of light is strong and just in front of the object. Here we see that it makes the sphere look flat. The middle is light in value, the borders are dark. This effect is created in flash photography when the flash is coming directly from the camera.

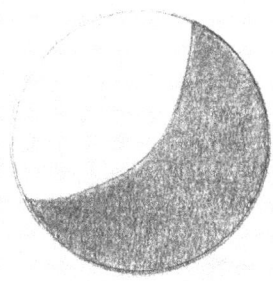

Form light describes a light coming from the upper or lower side of the object. It is called form light because it accentuates the form of the object.

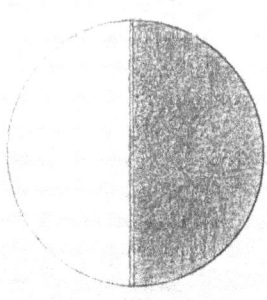

Side light is when the light source is shining on the object directly from the side. Here it makes one half of the sphere light and the other dark.

Rim light describes a light source from the back upper or lower side of the object. Only a rim of the sphere is light in value.

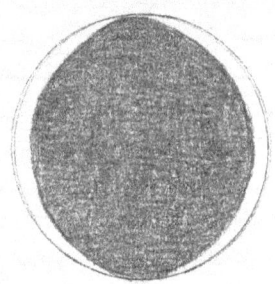

Back light means the light source comes from directly behind the object. On the sphere, we get a very light value on the borders only.

Regardless of where light is coming from, there are always areas of light and shadow on any object, face or surface. These areas of light and shadow will have different values within them.

SHADOW TYPES

Generally speaking, shadow is found on the area of the object furthest away from the light source. But if you look closely at the illustration on the next page, you will see that there are different aspects of the shadowed portion of any object.

You might think the darkest part of the shadow on the object would be the part furthest from the light source, but this is not true. Normally, light bounces off the surface on which the object sits, making that part a little lighter. This is called **reflected light**.

The darkest part of the shadow on the object is the **core shadow**. (Core means "middle, center or main.")

The shadow that falls onto the nearby surface is called the **cast shadow**. (This shadow is "cast" or "thrown" onto the surface.) The darkness of the cast shadow depends on the strength of the light source. The stronger the light, the darker this shadow will be.

The darkest section of shadow off the object is the **occlusion shadow**. (Occlusion means "blocking.") Here, where the object meets the surface, the light is most intensely blocked, thus the darkest value.

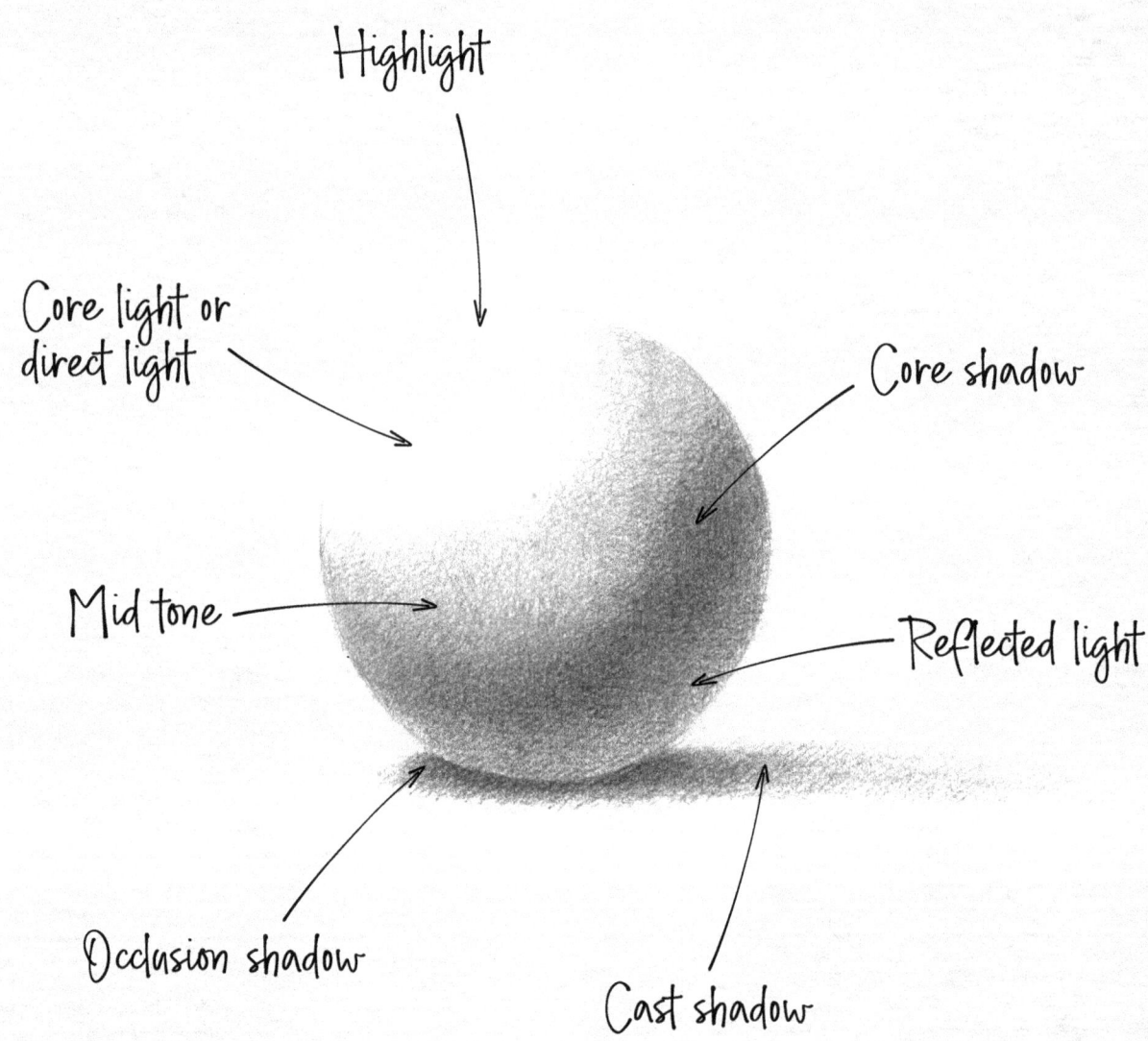

LIGHT TYPES

On the lighted side of the object there is also a part known as the **core light** or **direct light**. It's the part facing the light source, where light hits the object.

Next to this, the object becomes a little darker. This area is called the **mid tone**. It's an intermediate value between the direct light and the core shadow areas.

The lightest value, usually white, is a reflection of the light. It is called the **highlight**. It's usually the last part to add when you are drawing.

A TIP ON CAST SHADOWS

There is a simple technique for accurately drawing the shape of a cast shadow.

Draw two straight lines coming from the light source, touching the sides of the object, and continuing to the surface the object is resting on. The cast shadow would fall between these lines.

The angle at which the light hits the object determines the length and shape of the cast shadows. The lower the angle, the longer the shadow; the higher the angle, the smaller the shadow.

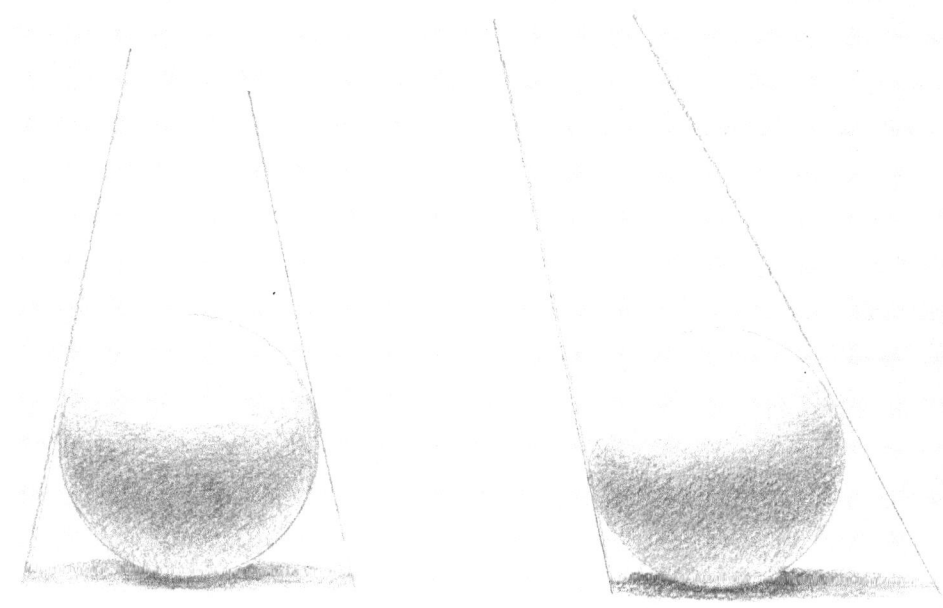

Remember, the darkest part of the cast shadow is sitting under the object.

Let's do This!

You will need:
- paper
- graphite pencils
- ruler

Draw or trace three circles.

Using the information on light source, the different parts of light and shadow, and how to draw a cast shadow accurately, draw three spheres with different light sources.

Think of the overall shape and appearance of each sphere as the light creates a different effect on each.

Let's do This!

You will need:
- paper
- graphite pencils
- ruler
- two geometric-shaped objects

Place the geometric objects in front of you and sketch them out.

Decide where the light source is coming from. Using the different shadow types and light types, make your objects look realistic.

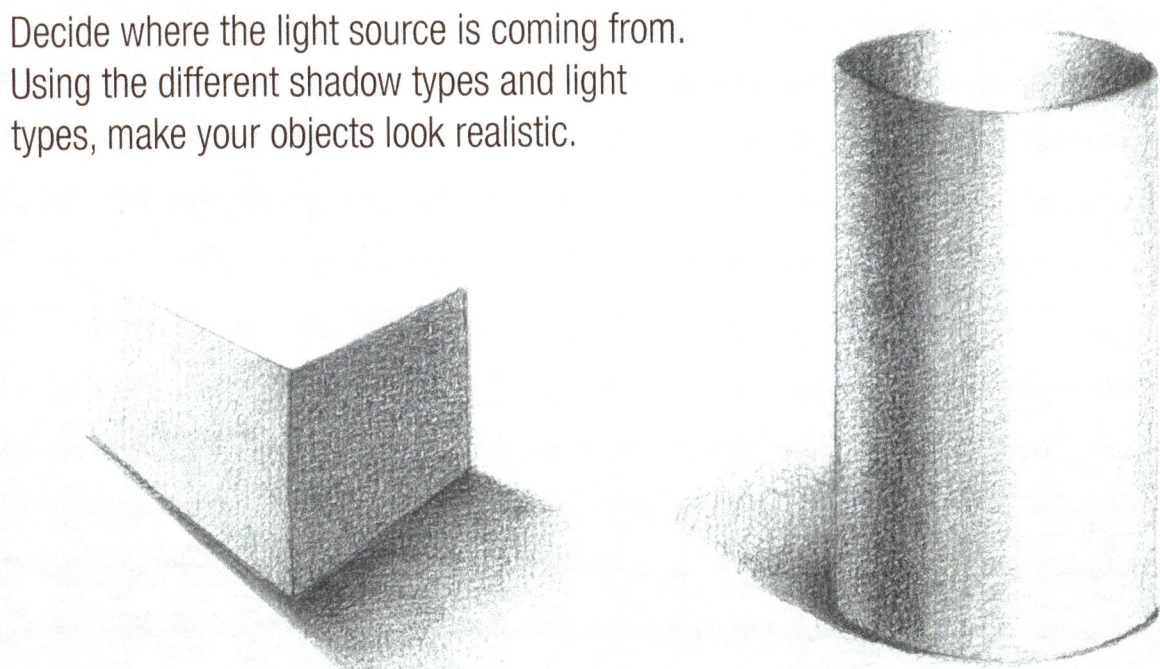

Let's do This!

You will need:

- paper
- graphite pencils
- ruler

Copy the outline of the drawing on the next page. Now decide where your light source will be.

In my example, I chose to have the light come from below and the side. I then continued asking myself, "Where would it be logical that light would hit the object directly and where would it not reach the object at all?" This guided all my lighting and shading decisions.

Based on where your light source is, fill in the light and shadow types, thinking with where the light would and would not fall, and how strongly.

Next, do it again, this time with the light coming from a different direction. If you wish, imagine the light brighter or dimmer than it was for the first one. As you draw, compare the second drawing with the first one and pay close attention to your value scale.

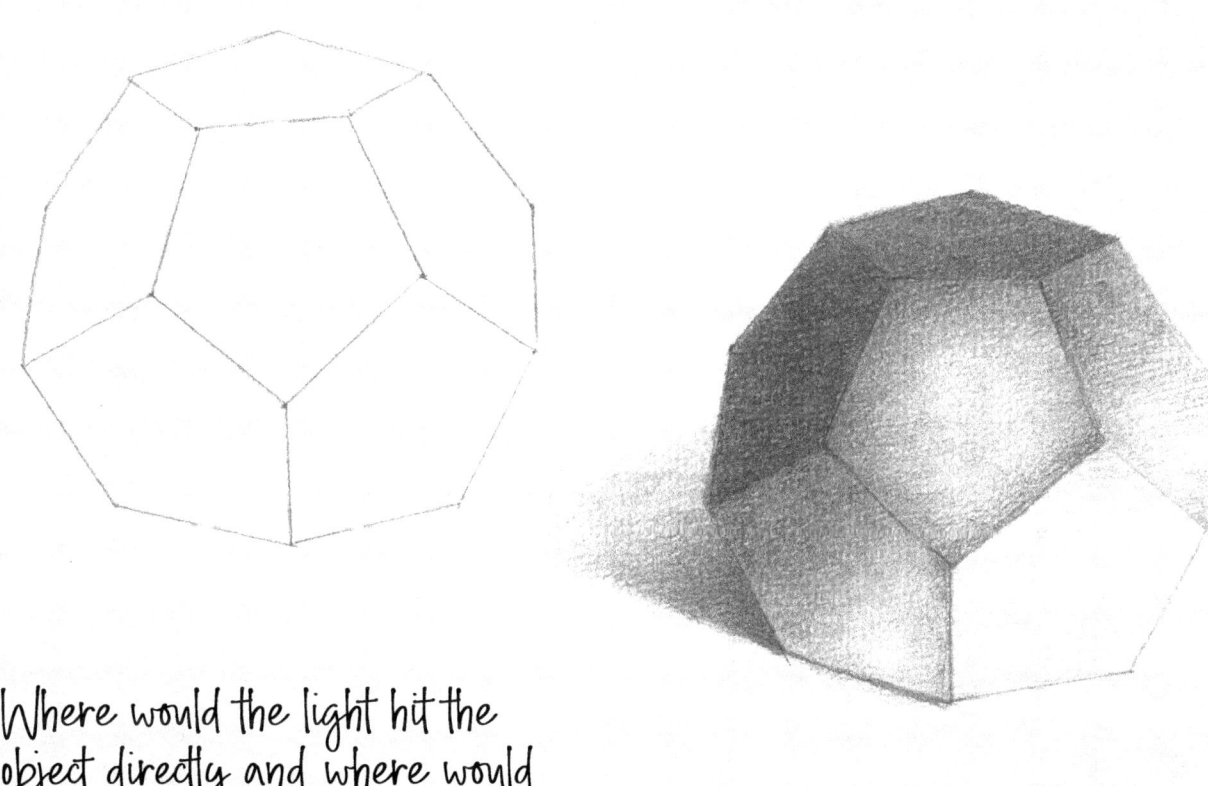

Where would the light hit the object directly and where would it not reach the object at all?

SEEING VALUES

Light affects everything it touches, but it takes practice to see the range of values created by light and shadow. When we are just learning to draw or paint, we often fail to see the different values in an object, person or scene they are drawing or painting. They tend to see only the shapes and colors.

Regardless of the shapes and colors, however, anything you draw or paint will have varied values depending on where it is in the scene, how the light is falling and reflecting, what's in shadow, and so on.

An example would be someone with light blue eyes whose face is half in shadow. Even though both eyes are light blue, the blue of the eye in shadow will have much darker values than the blue of the eye in the light. Painting them the same blue would not look right.

Another way to think about this is to imagine a sphere covered in white dots. These dots are all white, but they will look different depending on whether they are in the light or in the shadow.

The "white" dots will look different shades of gray where there is less light.

Here's another white dot example.

Light source

Darkest point

Notice the dots that do not have a white value but are shades of gray.

With practice, you will learn to see past the basic shapes and colors to the wide range of values in the things you are drawing and painting.

VALUE TRANSITIONS

Understanding value opens the door to drawing with great accuracy.

Another important aspect of capturing the correct values in your drawing is recognizing how values change or transition from light to dark or dark to light. These are called **value transitions**.

A square, metal pencil sharpener, for example, would have sharp edges and defined planes that would show sudden changes in value. There would be definite areas of light next to definite areas of dark.

Things such as boxes, chairs and buildings will often have sharp and sudden changes in value.

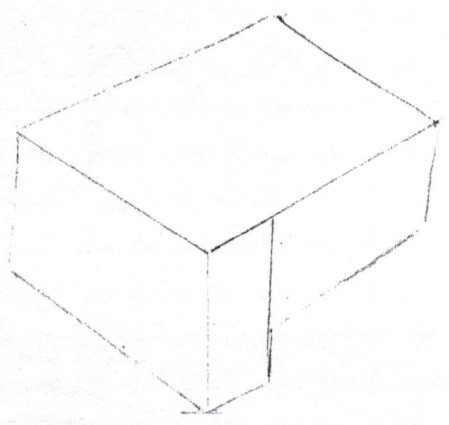
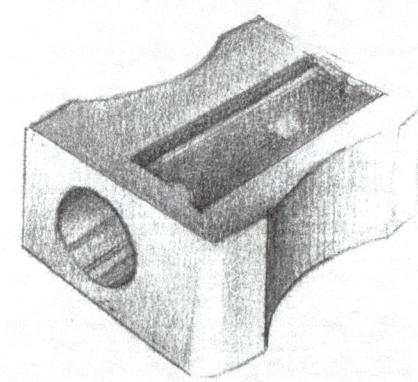

On the other hand, an object which has no sharp edges would simply flow from one plane to the next with a soft and gradual transition in value.

Examples would include such objects as clothes, faces or clouds.

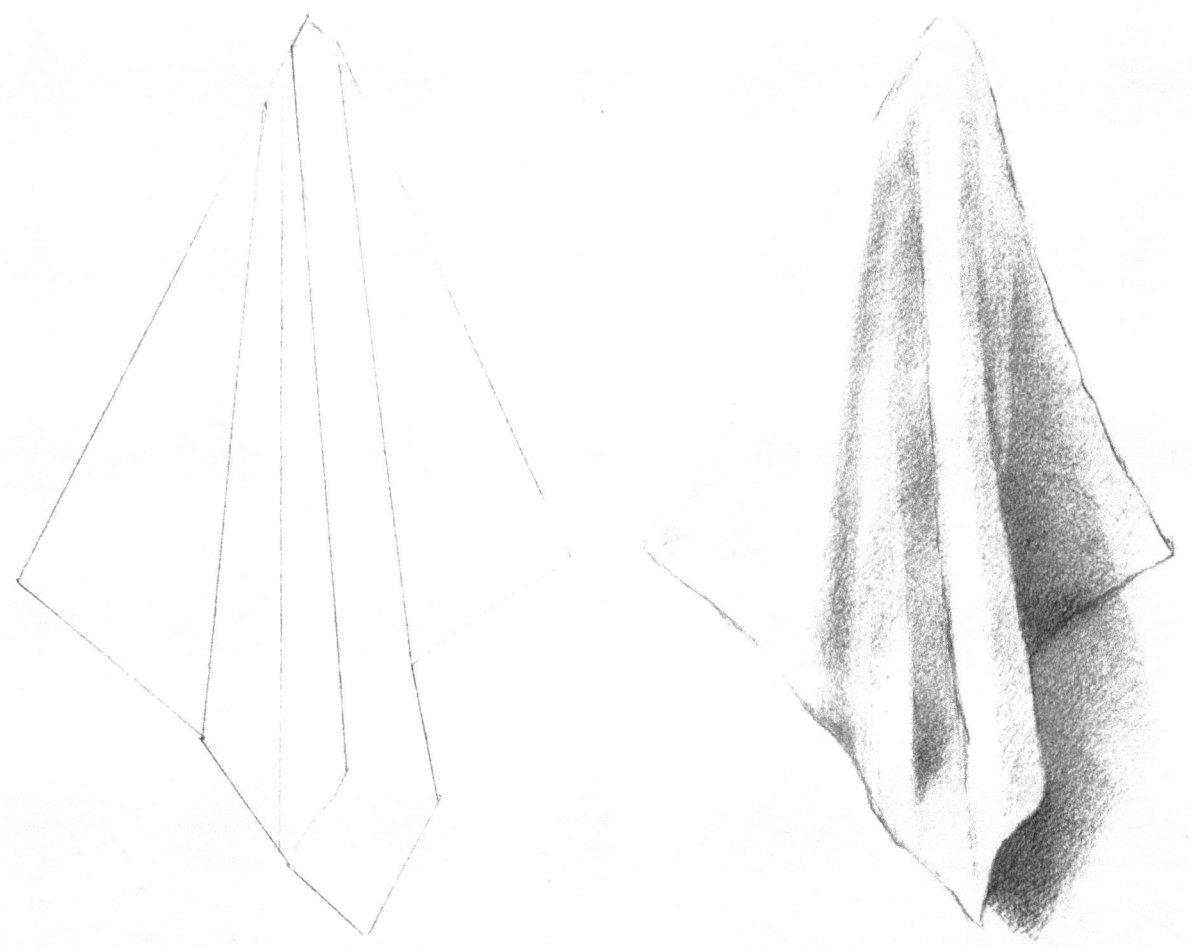

This drawing of a napkin shows gradual transitions in value.

Let's do This!

You will need:

   paper

   drawing pencils

Make a drawing of the crumpled paper on the next page. Start by drawing simple shapes to get the overall shape and proportions right.

Think about where the light source is and gradually add more detail, getting the values right in the different areas that are facing or away from the light.

As you do this, make sure the value transitions are smooth and accurately represent what you see.

Then repeat the exercise with the images on the following pages.

Both sharp and soft value changes.

Again, both soft and sharp value changes.

Notice the sharper, more extreme changes in value here.

Let's do This!

You will need:
- sculpture of a face
- lamp
- paper
- drawing pencils
- friend

For the first step, have your friend shine the lamp on the sculpture from many different angles. (If you have a lamp with a long, flexible arm, you can also do this by yourself.)

Look at which features become more pronounced under certain lighting positions and which seem to disappear or fade away. Does the emotion of the face seem to change?

Play with the light source to create different effects.

Choose a way to illuminate the face that feels good to you or that seems most interesting and leave the lamp in that position.

Make a drawing of the face with the light source position you have chosen.

Keep in mind everything you've learned about light, shadow and values!

COLOR AND VALUE

Imagine a red apple sitting on a table. The apple would always be red in color, but the top part where the light hits would be lighter in value while the part in shadow would have darker values.

You would have to paint lighter reds and darker reds to create a realistic-looking apple.

Every color has its own value scale.

The easiest way to change the value of a color is to add black or white. There are other ways to darken or lighten a color, but until you learn those, using white and black is a good starting point.

In all your art, whether it be color or black and white, incorporate all you've learned about value to create amazing pieces!

TWO INTERESTING ARTISTS

Maurits Cornelis Escher (1898-1972) was a Dutch artist most famous for his "impossible" drawings that include structures that look realistic but would be impossible to make according to the basic laws of physics and space.

He began his career drawing from nature and later found inspiration in buildings and architecture. Many scientists and mathematicians became fascinated by his works, which also found a broad popular audience throughout the world.

Most of his work was done as a printmaker, where his skilled handling of light, values, and vivid contrast was used to create fantastic realities of interlocking forms, objects turning into other objects, and architectural impossibilities.

Research

Find images of these pieces by M.C. Escher online:

    Print – *Bond of Union*

    Print – *Relativity*

    Woodcut – *Castle in the Air*

Rembrandt van Rijn (1606-1669) was also a Dutch master printmaker and draftsman (one who draws), but he is most famous for his paintings, which have been admired and studied by artists for centuries.

Extremely skilled as a painter, he is probably most revered for his ability to create atmosphere and mood through his dramatic interpretations of light and shadow.

In his many portraits, his work displays a penetrating intelligence, understanding and compassion for people.

He is considered by many the greatest portrait artist of all time. And through his dozens of self-portraits, one can feel his spirited presence as though he has not been gone four hundred years, but still lives with us now.

Research

Find images of these pieces by Rembrandt online:

    Painting – *Self-Portrait with Beret and Turned-Up Collar*

    Painting – *The Anatomy Lesson of Dr. Nicolaes Tulp*

    Painting – *The Storm on the Sea of Galilee*

ADDITIONAL EXERCISES

Let's do this!
Isolating values

You will need:

    red filter (red acetate value finder, red glass or red plexiglass)

This exercise has you look at different things through a value finder, or red filter, which makes the colors seem to disappear. Everything looks red, but the values (lightness and darkness) still show. This helps you see the values by eliminating the distraction of the different colors.

It makes the image or piece of art you are viewing **monochromatic**, which means one color (*mono-*, "one" + *chroma*, "color").

Walk around and look at people, objects and spaces with and without the filter, paying attention to the different values. Practice spotting the values without the filter and then comparing that with what the filter helps you see.

As you progress as an artist, feel free to use this type of value finder as a tool to more precisely identify the values in the subjects or scenes you are drawing or painting.

Let's do this!
Abstract art (values)

You will need:
- piece of card stock or sturdy paper
- scrap paper
- sheet of nice white paper
- piece of black charcoal, chalk or pastel
- scissors
- rag
- fixative

This is a messy but fun exercise.

Cut a shape out of the sturdy paper. You can draw it first or simply cut out any shape you choose. It should be no larger than your palm and it is best if it doesn't have fragile or narrow sections sticking out, as you will be rubbing it several times and they could tear off.

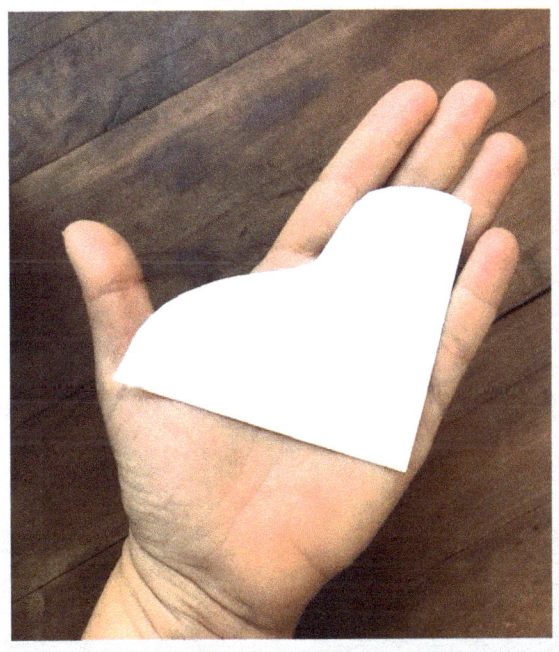

Place the shape on the scrap paper and using your black charcoal, draw a band of black all around the edge of the shape.

Now place the shape, charcoal side up, anywhere on your good piece of white paper. Holding it in the center so that it doesn't move around, use your fingertip to rub the black from the shape onto the white paper to create an edge all around it.

Use gentle but firm strokes. Do not rub back and forth. Instead, lift your finger after every stroke and rub again from the inside of the shape outwards. Go all around the shape.

Lift the shape carefully and place it on the scrap paper again.

Now repeat what you did two more times, making a fresh layer of charcoal around the edge of the shape, then placing it on the white paper so that it partially overlaps the first image. Rub the black outwards the same way you did before.

You now have three values on the paper. The white mark the shape left, the darkest part of the outline, and a lighter shade of dark as it fades out. Notice how the image seems to "pop" out of the paper.

Do these steps over and over, overlapping the shapes a little bit each time until you have filled the page.

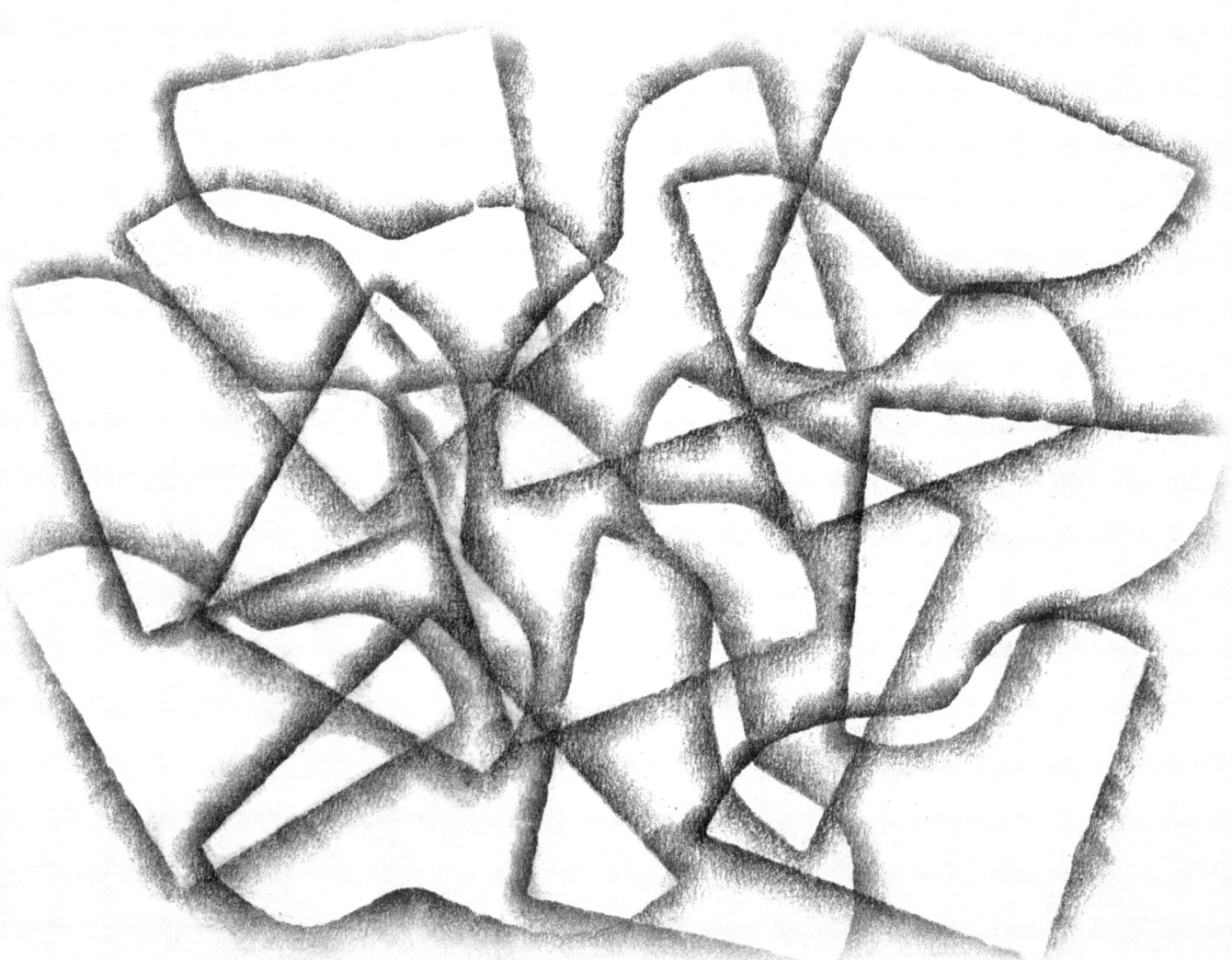

Spray your piece with a fixative so that it doesn't smudge.

Let's do this!
Cityscape (creating illusion of distance)

You will need:
- paper
- pencil
- black watercolor
- paintbrush

Have you ever noticed that objects appear lighter the farther they are from you? For example, the mountains in the distance look faded compared to objects nearby. By drawing or painting close objects darker and far-away objects lighter, you create the illusion of distance.

Make a simple drawing of rectangles next to each other, representing a bunch of buildings in a cityscape. They should have different heights and overlap in some sections.

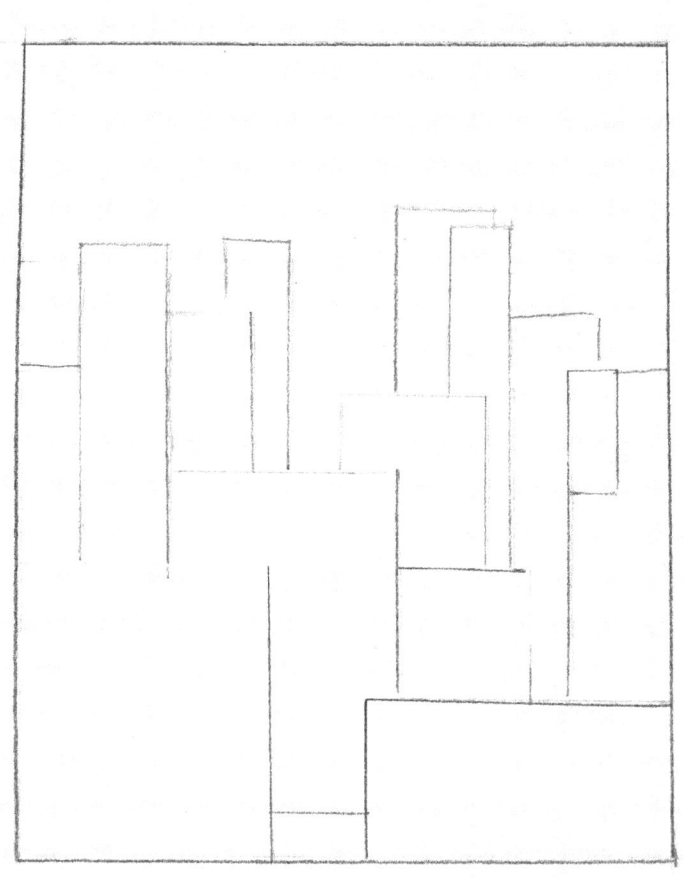

Using only black watercolor, paint the rectangles different values depending on how close or far away you want them to look.

Remember that to make watercolor lighter simply add more water. To make it darker, add more paint.

Start with the lighter values and gradually darken the sections you want to appear closer, observing the effect you create as you do this.

When you are happy with the result, you may add details such as windows, remembering to do them using values that match the buildings they are on.

Let's do this!
Abstract art (creating illusion of distance)

You will need:

    paper

    three pencils: light, medium and dark values

When there is no light source in the background, such as in a tunnel or a cave, you can create the illusion of distance by reversing what you normally do. In this case, make the values darker the farther you want objects to appear and lighter the closer you want them to appear. In other words, the furthest point would have the darkest value, and the values would get lighter as objects or surfaces get closer to you (or the viewer of the piece).

Using your lightest value pencil, draw some curvy shapes that fill your paper up, but make sure you leave a fairly thick border of the white paper in between each shape. Color them in with the lightest value pencil. Make the edges a little bit darker and transition softly towards the center of each shape.

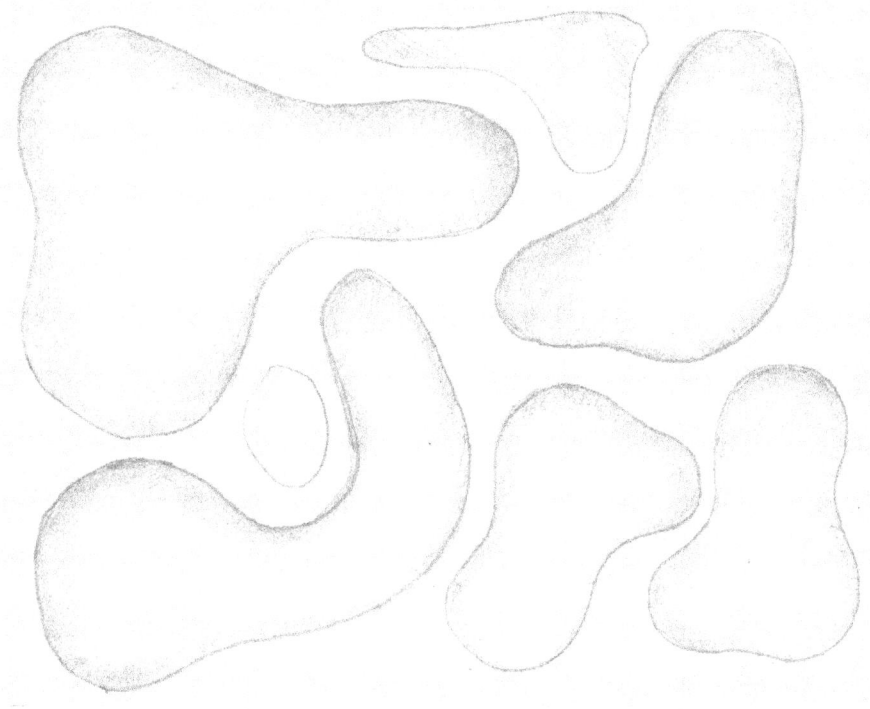

Now use your medium value pencil to draw shapes inside the first shapes. Make them so that they start inside one shape and look like they continue on to the shape next to it. Fill in this second layer of shapes with the medium value, again making the borders slightly darker than the middle.

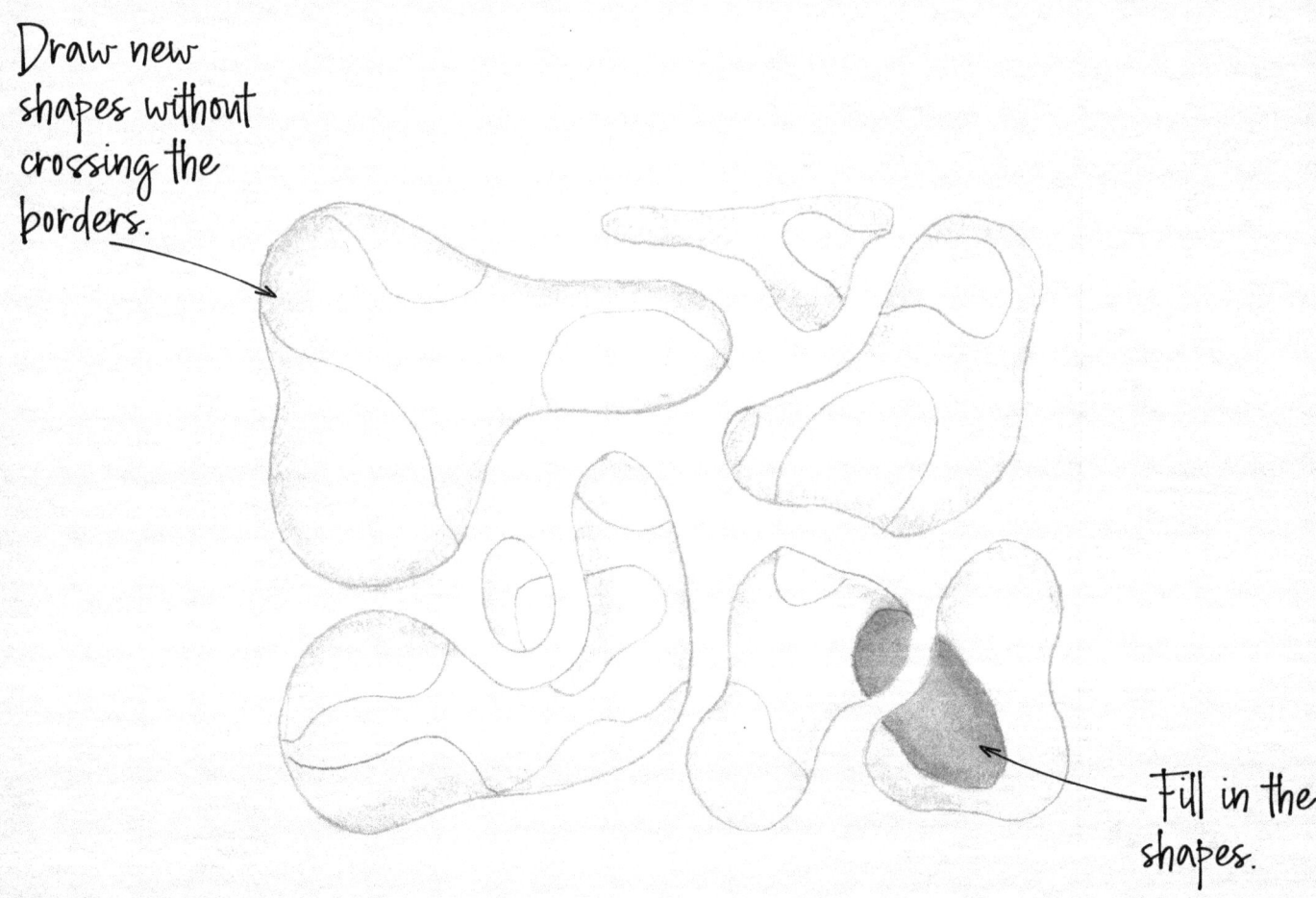

Draw new shapes without crossing the borders.

Fill in the shapes.

Next, using your darkest pencil, make a third layer of shapes. Draw new shapes inside the second layer of shapes. Again, without crossing over any space borders, make them look like they continue to nearby shapes. Fill this last layer with your darkest value.

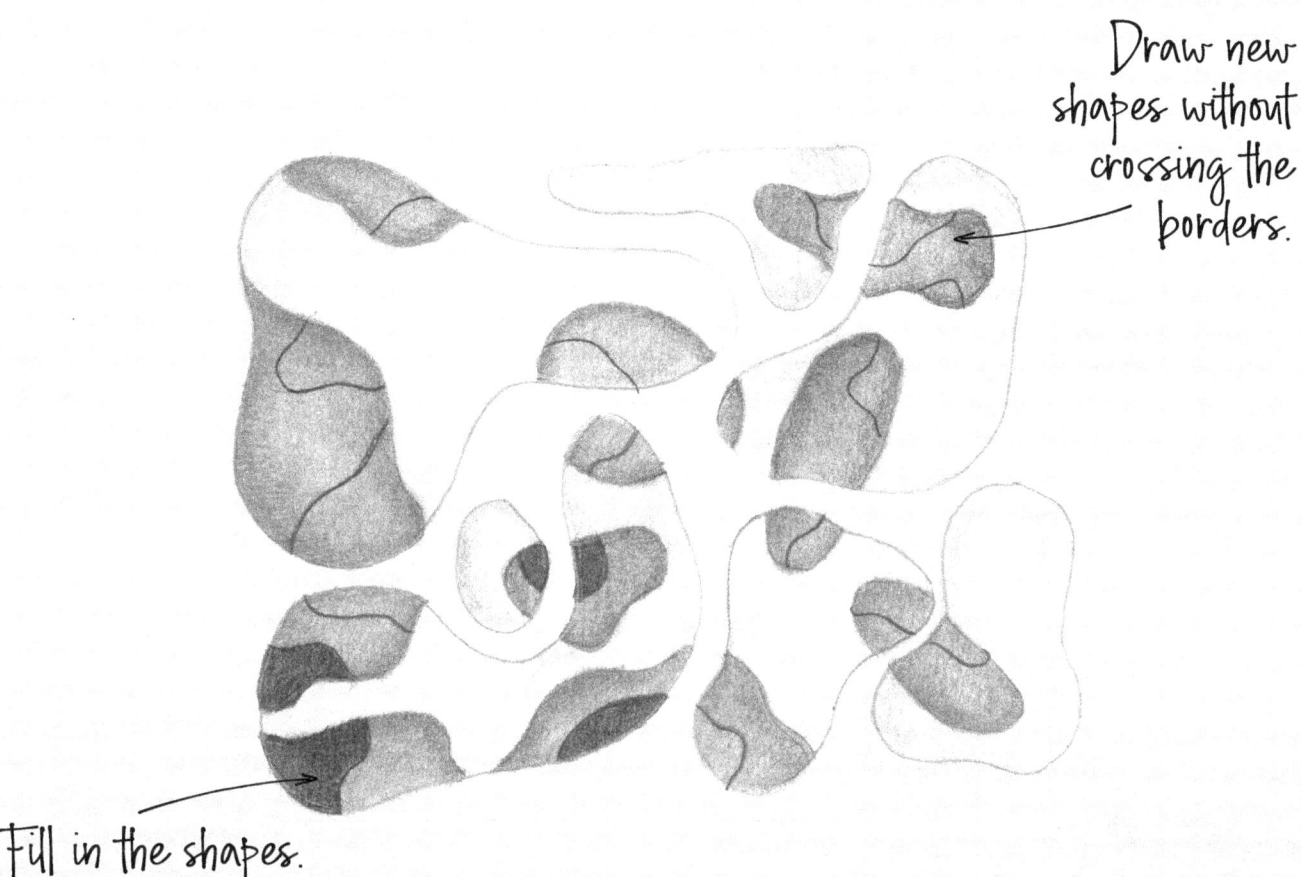

Draw new shapes without crossing the borders.

Fill in the shapes.

You can darken the borders with your dark pencil to make the work look crisp and clean.

Using only three values, you have made a very interesting art piece full of depth.

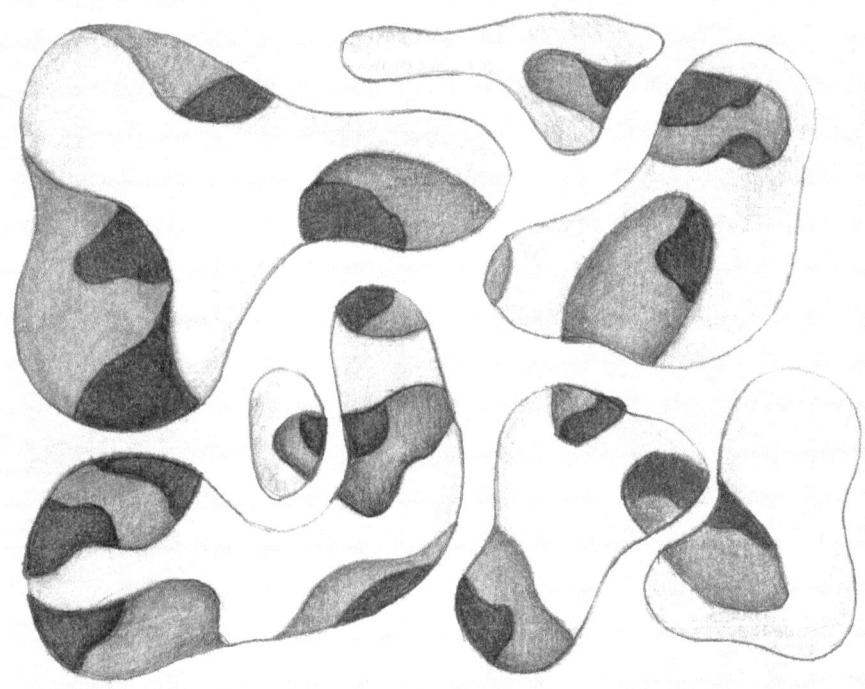

Let's do this!
Drawing a ribbon (light and shadow)

You will need:
- paper
- pencils
  - or
- watercolor paper
- watercolors

Using what you have learned about value, make a drawing of this ribbon.

Pay close attention to the different values and how they transition from dark to light as well as to the highlights.

Keep in mind where the light source is to help guide your decisions.

ABOUT NATASHA

An internationally exhibited artist, teacher and curriculum designer, Natasha Gray was born in 1969 in Mexico City. After completing middle and high school at the Delphian School in Oregon, which she credits with "opening my eyes to the wonders and beauty of study and learning," she went on to study fine arts at the Academia de San Carlos, the Art Students League of New York and the School of Visual Art in Paris. While in New York she worked under renowned Spanish artist Miguel Angel Argüello (1941–2005).

What followed was an eight-year pilgrimage into the ghost towns and deserts of the Southwest U.S. With only a small camper and paint supplies, she set aside all modern comforts to focus herself on studies of light and color, while honing her techniques and vision as an artist.

Eventually, Natasha returned to Mexico to raise a family. Over the ensuing years, she traveled extensively to study and exhibit her evolving work, which included creating pieces in a sub-genre of sculpture she calls "wire drawing."

In 2018 and 2019, Natasha decided to give back to the school where it all began by offering week-long workshops for students and arts faculty at Delphian, classes that spanned all grade levels. It was this work that inspired the collaboration with Heron Books to produce the *Natasha's Sketchbook* art instruction series.

The purpose is to provide simple, clear and joyful instruction in the elements of visual art. The goal is to help budding artists find the greatness of life and spirit within.

For more information visit natashagray.com.

Credits:

Adobe Stock:
p. 39 Blue eyes #330963953
p. 41 Pin up girl vintage #286765610
p. 45 crumpled tissue paper with clipping path #50001277
p. 46 3d Hanging White Towel #55130916
p. 47 abstract blue fabric in motion #262106682
p. 56 Modern living room interior #318513104
p. 71 Purple ribbon isolated on white background and texture #223685806

Rawpixel:
p. 3 Woman Holding a Balance (ca. 1664) by Johannes Vermeer #1015472

All other works are originals by Natasha Gray.

Since 1976, Heron Books has been pioneering the development of K-12 materials that foster creative, spirited learners who can use what they have studied. Books, courses and teacher resources are developed in collaboration with its sister organization, the Delphian School®, which routinely teaches four-year-olds to read and produces high school graduates increasingly sought by top universities and corporations.

Supported by subscriber fees, charitable gifts and book sales, the mission of Heron Books is

drawing out the best in every student.

heronbooks.com

Milton Keynes UK
Ingram Content Group UK Ltd.
UKHW051052121223
434220UK00010B/90